LIVES AND
TIMES

Mozart

Wendy Lynch

Heinemann Library
Chicago, Illinois

© 2000 Reed Educational & Professional Publishing
Published by Heinemann Library,
an imprint of Reed Educational & Professional Publishing,
Chicago, IL

Customer Service 888-454-2279
Visit our website at www.heinemannlibrary.com

Designed by Visual Image
Illustrations by Kathryn Prewett
Originated by Dot Gradations
Printed and bound in Hong Kong/China

04 03 02
10 9 8 7 6 5 4

Library of Congress Cataloging-in-Publication Data
Lynch, Wendy, 1945-
    Mozart / Wendy Lynch.
        p. cm. – (Lives and times)
    Includes bibliographical references (p.   ) and index.
    Summary: A simple biography of the man who composed such musical
works as "The Magic Flute."
    ISBN 1-57572-219-4 (library binding)
    1. Mozart, Wolfgang Amadeus, 1756-1791 Juvenile literature.
2. Composers—Austria Biography Juvenile literature. [1. Mozart,
Wolfgang Amadeus, 1756-1791. 2. Composers.] I. Title.
II. Series: Lives and times (Des Plaines, Ill.)
ML3930.M9L96 2000
780'.92—dc21
    [B]   99-37280
                                            CIP

Acknowledgments
The Publishers would like to thank the following for permission to reproduce photographs: AKG London, p. 19, E. Lessing, p. 17; Haddon Davies, p. 23; Mary Evans/Explorer, p. 16; The Ronald Grant Archive, p. 22; Her Majesty Queen Elizabeth II (Royal Collection Enterprises Ltd.), p. 20; Internationale Stiftung Mozarteum Salzburg, p. 18; Yiorgos Nikiteas, p. 21.

Cover photo: Rex Features

Some words are shown in bold, **like this**. You can find out what they mean by looking in the glossary.

Contents

Part One

The Story of Mozart 4

Part Two

How Can We Find out about Mozart? 16

Glossary...............................24

More Books to Read.......................24

Index.....................24

Part One

Wolfgang Amadeus Mozart was born in Salzburg, Austria, on January 27, 1756. When he was three years old, he liked to stand on a chair and sing songs for his mother, father, and sister.

Mozart watched his older sister Nannerl
play the **clavier**. He wanted to learn, too.
His father began teaching him to play
when he was four years old.

When Mozart was five, he began to make up his own music. This is called **composing**. Mozart could also play the **clavier**, violin, and organ when he was six.

Mozart did not go to school. His father taught him at home. He liked math and music best. He wrote math problems on blackboards on the walls of his house.

When Mozart was seven, he and Nannerl went on a long **tour** of Europe with their father. They played music for kings and queens and other important people.

Mozart was very ill while he was away from home. He caught **typhoid** and **scarlet fever**. These illnesses made him weak.

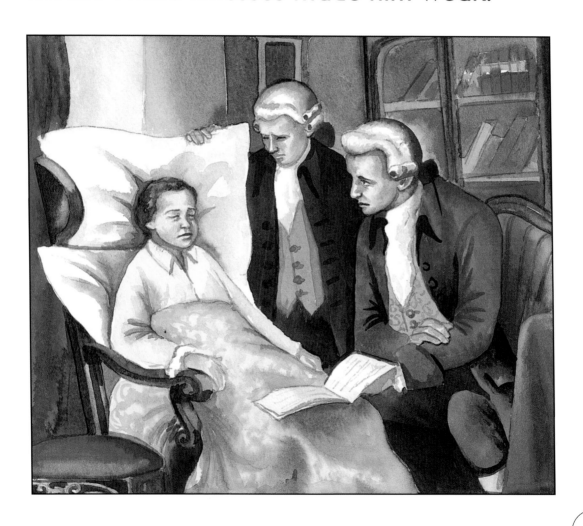

At the age of nine, Mozart wrote his first **symphony** for a whole **orchestra**. He also learned how to **conduct** an orchestra.

As he grew up, Mozart earned money by **composing** and playing music for rich and important people. These people were called **patrons**.

When Mozart was 25, he went to live in Vienna, Austria. There he married a woman named Constanze. They had a son named Franz, who also grew up to be a **composer**.

Mozart composed a lot of famous music in Vienna. He liked writing **operas** best. One of his operas is called *The Magic Flute*.

Mozart was paid money for his music. He and Constanze had a house with servants. But they were always in **debt** because Mozart spent more money than he earned.

Mozart died on December 5, 1791. He was only 35 years old. Many people thought Mozart was the greatest musical **composer** in the world.

Part Two

There are many ways in which we can find out about Mozart. We can look at paintings of him. Here is a painting of him when he was six, with his father and his sister.

You can visit the house in Salzburg where Mozart was born. Now it is a museum. In the house, you can see the **clavier** Mozart used to play.

Mozart wrote many letters to his family
and his friends when he was traveling.
Here is a letter that he wrote to his wife
in the year he died.

Many things were written about Mozart during his life. This is a poster advertising his **opera** *Don Giovanni*.

Here is a **manuscript** written by Mozart when he was eleven. It shows how Mozart wrote his music on the page. It also shows how he crossed it out to make changes.

Mozart's music is still played at **concerts** all over the world. You can listen to his music on a CD or on the radio.

Mozart and his music are as popular as ever. A movie about his life, called *Amadeus*, won many awards. Many people started listening to Mozart's music after they saw the movie.

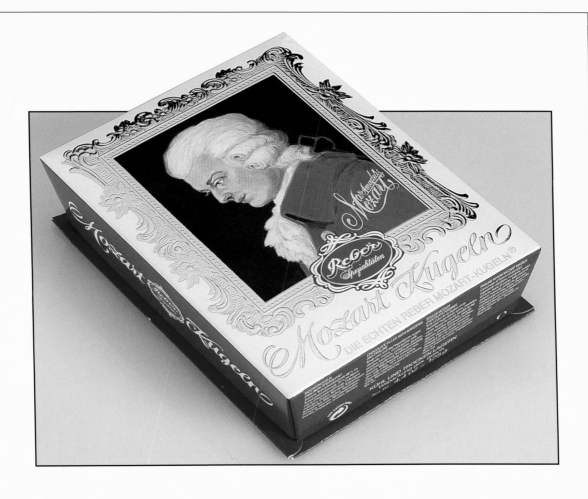

These chocolates are named after Mozart.
You can buy them in special candy shops
all over the world. This shows how
popular Mozart still is.

Glossary

clavier early type of keyboard instrument. You say *kla-veer*.

compose to make up music

conduct to direct an orchestra

debt owing more money than you can pay. You say *det*.

manuscript anything written by hand. You say *man-you-script*.

opera play that is sung, not spoken

orchestra large group of musicians who play together. You say *or-kes-tra*.

patron someone who gives money or support to a person or group. You say *pay-tron*.

scarlet fever bad illness that gives you fever and a rash

symphony long piece of music for many musical instruments. You say *sim-fun-ee*.

tour long trip to different countries

typhoid illness that gives you fever and headaches. You say *tie-foyd*.

Index

Austria 4, 12
clavier 5, 6, 17
Don Giovanni 19
illness 9

Magic Flute, The 13
marriage 12
opera 13, 19
patrons 11

Salzburg 4, 17
symphony 10
Vienna 12, 13

More Books to Read

Greene, Carol. *Wolfgang Amadeus Mozart: Musical Genius*. Danbury, Conn.: Children's Press, 1993.

Weil, Lisl. *Wolfer: The First Six Years in the Life of Wolfgang Amadeus Mozart*. New York: Holiday House, Inc., 1991.